Ernst Hofer

The School of Politics

The American Primary System

Ernst Hofer

The School of Politics
The American Primary System

ISBN/EAN: 9783337035242

Printed in Europe, USA, Canada, Australia, Japan

Cover: Foto ©Suzi / pixelio.de

More available books at **www.hansebooks.com**

THE SCHOOL OF POLITICS

THE AMERICAN PRIMARY SYSTEM.

By E. HOFER

Member 18th General Assembly, Salem, Oregon

CHICAGO
CHARLES H. KERR & COMPANY
56 FIFTH AVENUE
1896

New Occasions, No. 33.   Monthly, $1.00 per year.   March, 1893.
Entered at the Postoffice, Chicago, as second-class matter.

In the perfected nominating primary every member of every party should have a direct vote in the choice of every candidate whose name appears on the ticket of his party.

THE SCHOOL OF POLITICS.

THE AMERICAN PRIMARY SYSTEM.

An English critic has complimented the American people on their ability to think clearly and see straight. Applying this to the problem of good government, it is to be wondered how long before they will realize the absurdity of safeguarding the ballot-box and leaving entirely unprotected the nominating primary, a system under which the honest voter only too often ratifies the tools of corruption placed on the ballot for him, or he elects the corruptionist himself to offices of trust.

If it can be shown that the primary unit of our whole political fabric is defective, how can we attain good government, and how long can self-government by the people exist with this vital defect? Our political results become less and less representative.

One congress after another passes the billion dollar mark of appropriations, and our city governments and local legislatures are bywords for dissatisfaction.

Good government should be the expression in public affairs of the average intelligence, moral purpose and patriotism of a majority of the voters. If we consider the present system closely we will come to the conclusion that it has its beginning in the corrupt manipulation of the primaries and ends in a series of local and national struggles for spoils.

What is the most earnestly needed reform in American government? What is the greatest abuse connected with American politics?

Americans of all shades of political belief ask themselves this question at times. There are various answers. Finance and tariff, prohibition and Americanism are most common.

The belief that the American system is the best system of government has led the writer to enquire into its greatest defect in what follows. We are seeking to carry on a government of the people, by the people and for the people. We are seeking to avoid the dangers of socialism. But we are tolerating an abuse at the foundation of all our political activity that is leading us into aristocratic paternalism.

In what department of practical politics are the greatest abuses practiced? At the polls?

We boast of free and pure elections. In the court? We believe in justice. In the collection and disbursement of state and national revenues? Our system is almost perfect. Whence comes the great source of fraud and political corruption? *From the packed primaries, and manipulations of political machines rendered possible thereby all over our country.*

The criminal politics of our cities, that contain nearly one-third of the population of our country, extends into and corrupts our state and national government. The primary is the source whence springs all political power. If the source is vitiated, how can the stream of our national life be otherwise than impure, corrupting and finally destructive to our government? The answer to this inquiry is: *The corrupted primary is the political crime of the century.*

The spoils politician readily replies to all arguments for a reform in our system of holding primaries for nominating conventions, "How are you going to get the people to attend the primaries?" Let it be said, the people in any large numbers are not wanted at the primaries by the spoils politician. If out of a patriotic sense of duty they turn out in any number, these bosses for revenue see to it that they are not permitted any freedom of expression, that a slate is prepared for them, that the officers of the primary are there not to record the honest effort of the disinterested citizen but the dishonest effort of the interested boss. The primary laws in some of the states go so far as to compel the citizen to receive the printed ticket directly from the hands of the primary official immediately before he votes, and no other ticket is permitted to be used there. No real reform of this abuse is possible until the people are aroused to see that in allowing interested parties to conduct their primaries they are really surrendering their most important political privilege, the right to say who shall be the candidate of the party whose principles they espouse.

When it is said that the packing of the primaries ought to be stopped, we are met with the objection that the people will not turn out to vote at the primaries. Hence the boss is a necessity. He attends to these matters and gets out enough voters to carry his slates, and rewards himself out of the spoils of office by making up the ticket the people afterwards turn out well enough to vote. They consider voting a patriotic duty. But they dislike to take a hand in the management of practical politics, it is said. The term politician is odious. To refrain from meddling with politics is considered quite a virtue. So we have expensive campaigns to get out a full vote of the people to ratify a ticket that was put up by the action of one-tenth or one-twentieth of the party, that then becomes responsible for the actions of the few. In the large cities this leads to great corruption. A few men in each precinct are easily managed, and it has become so that only the few who want office are at all concerned in putting up a ticket and the so-called decent citizen stays away from the primaries entirely. Is it decent in a country attempting to conduct a government of the people for a voter to neglect his most important political duty? It is right here we find the cause of all that is indecent and corrupt in American politics.

It is not a question of ascertaining what is the greatest evil of American politics. It is how can we remedy it?

Civic duty implies patriotism, or love of country. It can not be performed by proxy. If only one-fourth of the virtue and intelligence of the community attends the primaries, where is laid the foundation of all that follows in the way of government and political results, why should we expect the result to be other than three-fourths bad? The one ward-worker who is out handling the primary machinery of poli-

tics counts far more than the three slippered
stay-at-homes.

It is plain we govern by proxy. The stay-
at-home voter delegates his political power for
bad government as surely as though he went to
the primary and cast his ballot for good government. He delegates it to the worst and most
unpatriotic. He gives his proxy to the boss.
The boss is an irresponsible despot. We have
not seen him at his worst. With the growth of
interests and increasing wealth we shall see him
lay his hands on the presidency and the supreme court. At times the people of a state
have arisen and tumbled a boss in the dust. The
occasional wreck of a boss is as nothing com-
paied to their growth in numbers and boldness.
"Punish the bosses" is a feeling that has grown
up in all parties and has often been acted upon.
But it is a costly and unsatisfactory remedy.
It is as defective in theory as locking the stable
after the horse is stolen. It was this last resort
of the voter, in his extremity seeking to strike
at the primal cause of misgovernment, that led
to the defeat of Folger in New York for gover-
nor in 1882.

In packing the primaries and forcing the
nomination of Folger by means of the machine,
President Arthur forced upon the country the

only alternative of defeating the party by that all-powerful and constantly more frequently resorted-to weapon, the stay-at-home vote. In 1890, 1891, and 1892, Republicans again rebuked their party by turning down their bosses. Pennsylvania, Iowa, Massachusetts, Michigan, Wisconsin, Oregon, and other strong Northern Republican states elected Democratic governors and some of them re-elected them, as well as other state officials. Nothing so effectually hurts the name of even a good political party as the reputation of bossism. By driving the disinterested citizen away from the primaries, millions of the best men in our country are kept away from the polls. The increase of the stay-at-home vote is one of the most alarming features of our political conditions. But so far there has been found no other effective way to punish the bosses. Defeating the party ticket to punish the bosses is like burning down a house to get rid of an obnoxious tenant. The people will endure bossism rather than punish themselves to get rid of it. The bosses are disposed to take advantage of the reluctance to apply the rod in 1896, and our country stands in danger of going into the hands of the worst class of American public men.

Can any intelligent American look back upon

past presidential campaigns with feelings of pride?

We do not refer to that large class of persons who regard politics as the science of government looting. We speak of Americans as well-wishers of their country, who have no selfish designs upon their fellowmen. Let such as are mere disinterested citizens, as far as the spoils of politics are concerned, contemplate the figures published about the expenses of the last two national campaigns. Two million dollars was spent in one state, or over twenty thousand dollars for each county. Four millions was used in the rest of the United States, and as much more was spent by the opposition. Three men in Pennsylvania raised a million dollars, and New York, New Jersey and Ohio contributed a million and a half more. In 1880 the national committees spent a million and a half each, of which half a million was spent in Indiana. A large volume of facts of this kind could be gathered about the national campaigns of the past twenty years. The beginning of all this vast expense is found in the cost of managing the primaries in the cities. Out of the prestige gained in this work very small men in ward politics in a few years rise to be figures of national importance. Ward-workers become receivers of transcontinental railroads, and bar-room beats become authorities on national politics. It will be said this is the glory of a democratic form of government. If it led to good government that might be a cause of pride. But that it leads to government by the worst, to the suppression of the best impulses of a free people, is a lamentable fact. The great issue in the national campaign is not the tariff or finance, but the question whether the administration shall be responsible to the people or to the bosses.

The most marked feature of the approaching presidential contest of 1896 is the decadence of issues and the prominence of the boss, the absence of principle and the presence of the machine. As in the Harrison administration the struggle was whether the executive council of the national campaign committee should be the governing power, or the president and his cabinet, so in the forthcoming campaign the bosses are fighting for the real rulership of the nation, no matter who is president. The preliminary contests have been waged with much virulence in states like Pennsylvania and New York, where Platt and Quay are put in power by the machine, and in Maryland and Ohio, where Gorman and Brice are enthroned. Be it Republican or Democrat, the issue is the same

—shall you be represented by a properly dele-
gated representative of the people or shall you
be ruled by the creature of a boss? Shall political power spring from the people or shall it
emanate from the manipulating of a political organization? This fight will be on in every state of
the Union. In every state where this is not
determined it will be inside of the next six
months. It must be determined rightly, or all
the fruits of the great victory Republicans expect to win in the next national election will
turn into poison for the commonwealth.

What blackened the name of Hayes? Bossism.
What ruined the Garfield administration and cost
him his life? The struggle of a few bosses to
run the administration. What prevented President Arthur's renomination and turned the
country Democratic in 1884? The rapacity of
the bosses,who were not even satisfied with one
of their own class, because they could not run
him. What class of men disrupted the Harrison
administration, attacked his right to be renomi
nated, and then by their indifference deprived
him of the enthusiastic support of his party?
The professional office-hunters,who are not satisfied to allow the people to progress and enjoy
prosperity.

We are living in an era of darkest bossism,

when the sun of free self-government by the people has nearly set. Both parties in this period are under the domination of the boss. The exact counterpart of each other in absence of character and ambitions for the real rulership of the nation, can be found in each party. As there is no difference in the political beliefs of the bosses, though in opposite parties, so there is no disturbance on the placid surface of their boss-ruled organization. But there is a muttering as of a volcano preparing for an upheaval in the depths of the voiceless masses. This deep-felt spirit of revolt is waiting for an opportunity to strike a death-blow at all that is most degrading in American politics. Bossism is conceived in corruption, born in crime, nurtured in extravagance, and reared in iniquity. Self-government is a delusion, the voice of the people expressed in public affairs a dream, and good government an impossibility, until a system that appeals to all that is worst in human nature is driven out of our politics. Bossism has laughed for twenty years at the pessimistic mouthings of mugwumps, and the abuse of pulpit politicians has only elicited its contempt. Bossism has been showing its hand in a score of states as an evidence of what it intends to do. It will seek to rule in national affairs and set up its dummy in Washington, or again bathe the national capital in blood. If it can carry out its plans it will seek to suppress the revolt in the hearts of the people, so as to be able to transfer its régime of corruption, incompetency and indecency from the cities and states which it has under its control to the government of the entire nation. Civic virtue and moral courage will be called upon to deal with this monster that threatens the national life.

Purification of the primary unit of our politics is absolutely necessary if we would not see our country go down into the worst quagmire of corruption that ever swallowed a republic. All the remedies of fragmentary statesmanship will be applied in vain so long as we allow the very source of all our political activity to be poisoned at the primaries as it is now done all over this land. Large sums of money are spent in nearly all large cities and in many of the county precincts to carry the party primaries for the slates of the bosses. This money is paid to the heelers and strikers to "rustle" the most ignorant and criminal elements from the slums, saloons and boarding houses for so much per head to elect certain delegates to the county conventions, which then make the ticket which the honest voter afterwards ratifies at the polls.

The money used for this purpose is advanced by the boss, often by capitalists or banks, contractors and corporations, and it is afterward paid back out of the public treasury, or out of the party's power to bestow offices, from positions in presidential cabinets to janitorships in public schools. While this is expensive and destructive to the public service, the fact that primaries held in this way are the expression of the worst passions of selfish and purchasable partisans, is the gigantic crime of the age, and the political dynamite that will surely and speedily blow the republic to pieces. Our country cannot depend upon an occasional Rev. Parkhurst turning up to pull it out of the mire of the consequent political corruption. The purpose of this writing is to strike at the very source of this primary evil and restore representative government to the hands of the people, where it belongs. When an American is hurt and knows what is hurting him, he wants to strike the thing squarely between the eyes. Our government is not a conspiracy between the wealthy and the wicked, as some would have us think. But it is the result of a combination between the selfish and the unpatriotic.

The importance of ascertaining what is the real unit of our political action must be apparent to all. If a great wrong is being done to the multitude by the sharp practices of a few, the sooner the many who are injured thereby unmask the wrong-doers and punish them the better it will be for the welfare of our country. If debts can be heaped upon our cities without limit, if legislatures become the cesspools of corruption, if boards of education become mere employment bureaus for incompetent persons who could not otherwise go upon the public pay-rolls, if out national congress has become the mere breeding place of plutocratic conspiracies, if our federal courts are merely to register the decrees of corporation wreckers,—if these practices are the ultimate purpose of American politics we might rest content with our achievements. But if we are unwilling to see a mere reproduction on American soil of the political conditions prevailing under the monarchies of Europe, our country governed by wealthy monopolists, with all the vices but without the character and culture of an aristocracy, we must purify at once the unit of all our political activity—the precinct primaries. If the integer of our calculations is rotten, what shall be the result? The past year the nation has been agitated by a discussion of "The Crime of 1873," to determine whether the gold dollar, the silver dollar, or both, shall be

the primary monetary unit. It is assumed that
in finance all depends upon the elementary unit
of the coinage. The character of the unit shall
be fixed by national law. It shall not be debased
or counterfeit. The coin of the realm shall not
be spurious. Be the volume in circulation great
or small, the fixed value of the unit upholds the
commerce of the world, and renders the highest
approximate justice possible in all transactions.
What is the unit of all our political activity?
Is it defined by laws? Is it composed of good
metal or is it debased and corrupted? Ask
yourselves, American citizens, are you the basal
unit of our politics when you go to the polls to
vote the party ticket, or are you the unit when
you attend the party primaries that make that
ticket? Perhaps you did not attend, but simply
intend to blindly ratify what is placed before you
on election day. We will assume that you did
attend the primaries, in your precinct. Were
you the unit of action there, as you should have
been, a constituent member of a popular republic? Or was there a slate made for you when
you got there, to save you all trouble? Per-
chance you had your choice of two slates, neither
of which you knew anything about? Yet by
voting one you placed just so much concentrated
political power in the hands of men who are

ready and willing to make you pay dearly for
their labor-saving devices.   There is not a little
expense getting acquainted with the people of
your precinct, of making that slate for you to
vote at your primary, of getting out enough
voters to carry your precinct, with voters who
are often of the lowest classes, or even foreign-
ers just naturalized for the purpose. But when
you went over and voted with them, they
and you, both classes ignorant as horses of what
is really being done, are the units of our political political system.   Do you wonder that you
are taxed until your property is a burden and
your business a failure? Are you surprised that
the laws are made to shield vices?   Are your
criminals pardoned, your police corrupt, your
schools a failure, your courts a farce and dis-
obeyed, and government a failure? The boss
tells you that if you don't attend you are to
blame.   We are conducting self-government by
the people.   You are one of the units of the
government.   You have failed to do your duty,
in your primary capacity.   The sum total of
such actions can only be failure.   But the boss
does not tell you that he conducts that primary,
or made the laws by which it was conducted.

Bossism is to-day the dominant force in our
politics.   Bossism is government through the

worst, and at the largest expense possible. It is
the result of two controlling forces in American
cities. One of the forces springs from the am-
bition of prominent and wealthy men to have
the honors and perquisites of official life, without going to the trouble to ask their fellowmen
to confer those honors. They want places on
commissions, boards, consulships and foreign
missions. They sometimes attain to the position
of state chairman, national ·committeeman, or
delegate to national and state conventions.
For all this they are expected to pay. The
second force that goes to make bossism is the
appetite of the office-seeking class. They want
offices for what there is in them. The wealthy
partisan for honor and the enterprising for revenue strike hands. But there is another man
needed to carry their force into effect. It is the
boss. Sometimes the boss is himself a candidate
for a lucrative office, but seldom for honor.
Most frequently the boss is too corrupt and must
engage in practices too risky to be available for
public office, but he is frequently appointed to
positions of honor and emolument after the party
battle is won. Such are most of the collector-
ships, police commissionerships, superintendents
of public institutions, and postmasters in larger
cities. But the great public offense of bossism

is the conversion of the policeman from a
peace guardian into a protector of gamblers,
prostitutes and ward politicians, the transfor-
mation of the courts from instruments of justice
into compounders of crimes, and the changing
of banks from places for safe-keeping public
moneys into organizations for wholesale defal-
cations. In smaller ways the corrupting rami-
fications of bossism extend to the humbler
inhabitants, the laborers, the draymen, the street
sweepers, undermining public sentiment and
public virtue in a manner dangerous to the lib-
erty and conscience of the people. Once in a
while a nest of corruptionists is unearthed by
chance and dragged into the courts, and unable
to defeat the laws entirely, heavy fines are im-
posed. The bosses or their creatures make a
"raise" among capitalists or bankers, and again
go to work to restore their fortunes out of the
public service. It is stated openly that the
opium and the Chinese smuggling ring in a
large city expended a hundred thousand dollars
in this way the past year, and must recoup itself
out of the campaign of 1896. The principal
sufferer from a spasmodic application of justice
in the federal courts says he cannot make his
money back in any office but that of sheriff, and
that office he must have. As he is one of the

few men who can handle the tough element in the wards of the city at the primaries,there seems to be no way under the boss system of politics but to let him go in and make his money back. As he owes his fine to the banks and his expenses of trial to the lawyers, these highly respectable elements of society cannot refuse to permit him to handle the primaries. As many of the weak banks are debtors to the public treasury in large sums and the strong banks make a great deal of money out of manipulation of the taxes and public warrants, they become the conservative bulwark of bossism in a political campaign. When it is remembered that the same bosses, beginning in the primaries, make the United States senators and through them make the federal courts, where these same bosses handle the receiverships of the wrecked banks and corporations, it will be seen that bossism is to day the dominant force in American public affairs. The business man and private citizen who remains away from the primaries, or allows his name to be put upon the slate of delegates as a guaranty of good faith and respectability to enable thugs and boodlers to handle the county convention, can see just how he contributes to the upbuilding of public morality and good government in the name of his party. Matthew Arnold com-

plimented the American people for their ability
to think clearly and see straight. But can they?

Self-government by the people is on trial.
The people want the best. The masses have no
interest in anything but good government.
When they vote at the polls they do not knowingly vote for corruption and extravagance.
They do not knowingly and intentionally
put bad men in office. The theory of a people's
government does not embrace the idea of the
enrichment of the few and the impoverishment
of the many. Yet that is what our government
is tending to become more and more. During
the past few years of depression and hard times,
the salaries of the official classes have not been
diminished. Congress after congress has ap-
propriated over a billion of dollars, and even the
expenses of the supreme court have increased
from three million five hundred thousand dollars
to over five million dollars. The standard-oil
magnates and the sugar-trust kings have rolled
up their increasing millions of profits yearly in
spite of the distress of the farmers and laborers
who had to buy their sugars and oil. They
have donated millions to the great colleges, and
Stanford has alone planted a colossal university
on the Pacific coast, but its catalogues are not
filled with sons of toil, or the farm, but with

the children of the already wealthy. These universities, unless placed on a democratic basis, will only widen the chasm between capital and labor. The combination in American politics, between corporations, capital and corruption, makes a mockery of the proposition that all men are created free and equal, and imposes on the masses all the oppressions possible under the old feudalism and all the galling inequalities between man and man practiced by any landed aristocracy. Unless the people can win back the right to delegate their authority and enforce representative responsibility from the first inception of the primary, or caucus, to the highest nominating convention, and office-holders in general, we shall see built up in our country a plutocracy consisting of wealth and power gained by corruption, and trampling under foot the last vestige of the liberties of the people.

So long as the primaries are left open to manipulation of interested parties there will be no separation of city, county, state and national government. Even the school election is made to contribute its quota of spoils to the machine, and teachers are appointed and traded into places by means of the political "pull." The city primaries are packed to secure county offices and state appointments. The federal patronage

is used to build up the heelers, who in return are
to help make a slate in the contest for state
offices and legislatures. So wheels revolve within wheels until the ordinary citizen is amazed
at the confusion and intricacy of the political
machinery which he is supposed to manage.
But the main wheel that drives all the vast and
complicated mechanism of American politics is
the unprotected primary. We protect the ballot-
box, the treasury, the courts and some minor
departments of government from selfish attacks
of interested parties. But we leave the primary,
the source and mainspring of all our political
procedures, to the control of the governing class,
who are interested not in the governed and still
less in good government. We all understand
that the bosses are not in politics for their health,
that their business is political trickery and ras-
cality; yet we expect the men they nominate to
be honest. Everybody knows where the ser-
pent of evil lies, but no one has been able to
scotch it. The Australian ballot has made it
impossible to vitiate the result of an election by
fraud or bribery. No man or set of men can be
elected to office under that law without a delib-
erate act of electicism on the part of the voter.
Still it looks as if an honest city government
were hopeless to expect. Honest men cry out

against the ever rising tide of corruption that
threatens to swamp our land, and ask that God
may have mercy on their souls for the rotten
deformity of their handiwork. While we have
the Australian ballot, it cannot be said that
we have perfected the election laws as has been
done in England, where in an important parlia-
mentary contest the polls are kept open for five
days. But we have left what is far more important—the nominating primary entirely unguarded by law, or guarded by laws drawn up
at the instance of the bosses themselves and for
their own protection. With our local county,
state and general elections all inter-meshing and
often held at the same time, the manipulation of
the primary becomes five-fold more important
to the man who has his living to make out of
politics. When he is left to place his own esti-
mate upon the importance of his service, is it
any surprise, whether honestly or dishonestly,
he places it sufficiently high? If he sets in mo-
tion the wheel that drives all the other wheels
in the mill of politics—the primary—why shall
he not take sufficient toll? When we have re-
formed the primaries so that no man shall govern
us without the consent of the governed, when
we have separated local, state and federal elections so that one boss cannot, by manipulating

one set of primaries and nominating convention,
control our affairs from the school district to the
president's appointments, then can we be said
to have a self-government by the people, and
not until then shall we be able to have honest '
officials, if by that time we have not so corrupted the masses of the people that we shall
have no honest citizens left. When the sheriff
who draws the jury and the judges on the bench
no longer owe their places to the machine, we
may be able to convict the man who has worked
the machine to corruptly enrich himself and
others. Even though local and general elections be held separate as to time, so long as the
present primary system prevails, they are held
under one machine and the people get but little
benefit from voting at different times for state,
city and school officials. We must either abolish the present delegate convention and primary,
or we must safeguard it by laws as stringent as
the ballot laws, provide for holding the primaries
at public expense and have a direct vote of all
parties for their choice of candidates at the
same time and place.

One of the concomitants of bossism is the
necessity forced upon all who go into politics
under this system of recouping in every way
out of the public treasury. Not only must they

oppose all economy in administration, all reduc-
tions in salary or the number of employés, but
it is fatal to the public service, as it induces the
office-holding class to shamefacedly give places
to as many of their own families and relatives
as possible. This accounts for presidents, cabinet ministers, heads of departments, senators,
congressmen, and all state and county officials
appointing their sons, daughters, wives and con-
nections to the tenth generation. The employment of all the patronage of an administration
to secure the passage of a bill through congress,
or to defeat one, is only an employment of the
same pernicious, degrading influence that begins
with manipulation of the party slate at the primary. This plan of recouping and speculating
out of political positions and profiting out of
political activity is extended to the sale of lots
in town sites platted by officials in the war department to every laborer who gets two dollars
a day on the government works. Superintendents of mints organize mining companies and
sell the stock to the employés under them.
Traffickers in spoils only use one position to build
up for another, and the public service becomes
a step-ladder by which the most aggressive spoil-
mongers mount to higher station and the whole
principle of promotion as a reward of ability or

actual leadership of the people is cast to the ground. When the spoils system forms a part-nership with the corporations to control the poli-tics and run the government of our country, we have a combination out of which must grow an in conceivable degree of public corruption, a system under the operation of which the last vestige of popular government and the last dream of free institutions pass into oblivion.

Our country has been besieged with reform-ers and reform parties that sought to educate the masses to demand better things, but none have struck at the root of all that is wrong in our po-litical system—the defective and often corrupted unit of all our politics, the nominating primary, the weak spot in our economic armor, where the poison enters in that undermines the entire result. The source of our politics does not spring from the people themselves and is not responsi-ble to them. There is a divided responsibility. The official is elected by the votes of people whom he should serve, but he is nominated by those who prey off the people. While he should be responsible to the public service and answerable for a good business administration of affairs, he complies with these reasonable demands only as a matter of form and, if he is an honest man, as politics goes, is loyal to the managers who make the slates first, and good government afterwards. His success in politics depends not upon a faithful discharge of duty to the people, but to the political bosses. This will be so until the power to fix nominating slates and pack conventions is taken away. Until the Australian ballot was invented men were voted in blocks at the general elections. That evil is done away with, and now all corruption is centered on the unprotected primary. The American people should not leave the primaries and nominating conventions open to manipulation of the selfish and designing element in public affairs, when they jealously guard the more or less corrupted result of those primaries at the ballot-box. Why the reform elements have so entirely overlooked this fact is a mystery. What is known as the "Staten Island basis of union" is now the *summum bonum* of all that is thought desirable by the various faddists. They demand the referendum, abolition of monopolies, direct election of presidents and senators, equal suffrage, land tax, prohibition and finance reform. They should know that the greatest obstacle to procuring any of these reforms is the primary in our larger cities, which are managed by the very elements that are opposed to every principle of reform that is asked for by patriotic men

and women.   In selecting a legislature the boss
always conducts a still hunt.   A sharp scrutiny
is kept of the men likely to be nominated in all
the legislative districts of the party in the majority.   He does not want men of known views or
decided preferences.   A man who will accept
a clerkship for a relative, a position in some
state institution, or an appointment under the
federal government is preferable.   If he will in
addition vote blindly for the measures of the
boss, he becomes doubly valuable and his services will be remembered even unto the third and
fourth generation.   For some such service sometimes a whole family are quartered on the party
and the people for twenty or thirty years.   Such
instances of reward for loyalty to bossism are
numerous in every state in the Union, and men
are serving in sinecures at Washington whose
fathers before them closed their eyes and voted
blindly either through ignorance or self-interest.
The patronage disposed of at one session of a
boss-ridden legislature mortgages the public service at high prices for several generations.   By
discounting the spoils not yet in its grasp, the
boss system extends the pernicious rule of its ad-
herents far into the future, and only death or an
uprising of the people can break its course or
interrupt its career.   Thus men like Quay and

Cameron have held on in a great state like Pennsylvania, when the one was supposed to have outlived his usefulness and the other his virtues. The last time Cameron was chosen senator his name was scarcely mentioned as a candidate, while other able men were brought before the people for the office. After the legislature was elected it was found that a majority were secretly pledged to return him to the senate, and it was done. Legislators who had not dared to go openly before the people as Cameron men, delivered their votes and received their reward when they were out of reach of their constituents. Thus men are elected to the highest legislative body in our government, who themselves would never go before the people for approval on their public record, by the votes of legislators who have surreptitiously tricked the people for their franchises.

The attempt to identify misrule with any religious organization must prove a failure. The political crime and corruption of the American people cannot be laid at the doors of any church. It must be laid at the doors of our national weakness—the desire to profit out of political activity, gain as the only motive of our public life. Bossism attacks American citizenship and American institutions at its weakest point—money-making from office-holding. But when it is remembered that all the money spent in packing primaries, fixing slates, managing conventions, in city, county, school, congressional, judiciary and national campaigns, must be recouped out of the people through the public service, it will be seen that the greatest incentive to corruption arises not from the actual cost of office-holding, but from the greater costs of office-getting, and then often the added expenses of investigation and litigation, in all of which the effort of the manager is to come out with a clean record at any cost. This system, which is peculiarly American, cannot be justly laid at the doors of ecclesiasticism. The boss in our city and state governments may find it convenient to make deals with a religious denomination. There are bosses of all parties that are Catholic and whole city governments that are Catholic on the boss plan. And so there are of other denominations and no denominations at all. In proportion as the masses of the people are poor and crowded together, if there be no restraining hand to compel the purification of the primaries, will the selfishness of the ambitious politician prostitute our politics for the purpose of gain. Twenty-eight millions of city population acting under the manipulation of corrupt bosses is a menace to free institutions that can never be provided against by all the virtues of a rural population. The struggle in every legislature is to secure the passage of bills that shall restrain the corruption of municipal politics. Many cities have given up the struggle and threaten the assessors with lynch law if they do not keep down the valuations, as the boodler politicians stop only at the constitutional limit in their raid on the taxpayers and in many cities even that limit is not a restraint.

THE NEW YORK PRIMARIES.

NEVER has the struggle for the control of primaries raged so fiercely as in New York in the late autumn of 1895. The reform wave of 1894 had exhausted itself, and after the moral elements had consented to a fusion with the machine, the work before the "easy boss," as Platt is called, was easy enough. Of course Tammany was victorious in the city, and Platt had the legislature. But there was yet the party organization for the presidential election to make sure of. Primaries had to be held to elect a new county central committee. By securing the chairman of this committee, the party machinery that grinds out the delegates to the national convention, and enables Mr. Platt to dictate the vote of New York in the nomination of president and vice-president, is placed in the hands of that boss of the Empire state. As soon as the reform movement was decently buried, Mr. Platt had a new enrollment of the party ordered to be taken on Saturday night, Nov. 23, 1895, between the hours of seven and ten o'clock.

There are 1,392 election districts in the city. The bureau of elections had changed the boundaries of many of these districts the previous summer so that many Republicans did not know in which district they lived, and the enrollment was held at places so obscure as to be difficult to find even by voters well known in the district. Only those whose names were down on the books after this brief one-evening enrollment could vote at the primaries held ten days later, and so Mr. Platt had an easy victory. With his followers in control of the enrollment, with the rolls packed with many names not properly belonging there, with his men again in charge of the December primaries, is it any wonder that his man, Lauterbach, was able to carry 21 out of the 35 assembly districts, even against a strongly organized opposition? Is it any wonder that Mr. Platt will be able to play the part of dictator in the national Republican convention, and secure for himself recognition with a cabinet position, and ample protection for the interests he represents? It should be remembered that the primary in New York City is not obligatory, but is subordinated to the customs of voluntary political organizations, the rules and by laws of which are paramount. Only on request is the primary put under oath.

Although only one to three hours were taken on a busy Saturday night, Nov. 23, in New York City, over 75,000 were reported as enrolled for voting at the primaries of Dec. 10th. In a majority of the 1,392 election precincts the enrollment exceeded the total Republican vote cast at the exciting election but a few weeks before. At no time in the last quarter of a century had so many as one half of the party been enrolled for the primaries. The rolls were systematically padded by the machine in the interest of a large representation to the state convention of 1896, that elects the national delegation and thus secures control of the patronage of the Empire State for four years to come. It was openly charged that one-fourth of the enrollment was fraudulent, and the campaign committee of the New York Republican club issued an address charging that "the enrollment of Nov. 23rd was in many instances improperly, if not fraudulently, conducted, and that in a large number of election districts many names have been added to or retained upon the rolls in violation of the constitution of the party." In an address to the chairman of the county Republican committee, who managed the enrollment, the following words are used: "We protest against the primaries being held under the present enrollment. Is it not manifest that if fraudulent and bogus rolls are used at the primaries there must follow fraudulent and sham organization which will be discredited by all the people, and will be useless for all purposes except as a machine to elect spurious delegates from this city to the conventions to be held during this year?" But the enrollment made Nov. 23rd was not revised. The primaries were held with that enrollment and were satisfactory to the Platt-Lauterbach machine. The above protests were issued over the names of the most distinguished Republican citizens of New York. The padded enrollment in the back rooms of saloons, made late Saturday night by interested spoilsmen, determines the politics of New York and the nation far more than any election at the polls that will be held the next four years or until such a basis of organization shall be overthrown.

Richard Croker and George B. McClellan discussed a movement for open primaries in New York City in December. Both of these Democratic leaders seem to realize that the old ninety-minute back-room secret caucus is a disgrace to American politics and a parody on self-government by the people. Tammany bosses that they are, their common sense tells them an all-day open primary, at which all members of their

party who chose to do so could register and de-
clare their choice of delegates or candidates
without intimidation,obstruction or fraud, would
at least be fair and American as a proposition
of common justice. These men are practical
politicians, and they realize the value and the
importance of a full and free expression of the
party as against a repressed and manipulated
expression. They frankly say that such an
all-day free open primary, at which all Demo-
crats, regardless of the fact whether they were
Tammany, could vote, and have their voice
counted in the make-up of county and state conventions, would "hurt somebody." The abolition
of abuses always hurts somebody,as the practice
of those abuses has made millionaires of such
men as Tweed, Platt and Croker. The open
all-day primary would do away with a manipulated partial enrollment of all parties,the packed
primaries and the slated conventions and combinations that follow, as night follows day. If
we are Americans and love fair play, let us go
a step farther and hold an all-day primary for all
parties at the same time and place in each election
precinct, at which every member of each party
can go and vote directly for his choice of delegates or candidates from constable to president,
and we shall have struck at the upas-tree of cor-

ruption that now poisons our political institutions at their very inception.   If men like Croker can say,let us have an all-day open primary for Tammany and the Democratic party, we can say let us have a primary for all alike, regulated by law, paid for by the public, for all parties at once. The result of the false New York enrollment and illegal primaries is to taint the entire representation to the national conventions. The leading papers say that enrollment should be utterly swept away and the fountain purified. "The enrollment lists were stuffed beyond recognition by the heelers previous to the primaries." "A living picture of naked depravity," is what the New York *Mail and Express* calls it,and demands that the enrollment be purged of the names of "Tammany men, convicts, women, children, cats and dogs," which were massed to give the Platt-Lauterbach combination an overwhelming control in the coming New York State Convention. The primaries in New York are probably not more closely connected with criminal politics than in other large cities, but New York has a dominant influence in national affairs.

In New York the party primaries can only be subjected to legal regulation upon written application of five voters of the election precinct.

Then the officers of the primary can be put under
oath and must keep a record of the votes cast,
and frauds are punishable under the provisions
and penalties of the election laws. But as the
enrollment precedes the primary, and none can
vote who are not enrolled, and as both enrollment and primary are entirely under control of
the boss, the New York law is only a protection to the corruptionists.

The representation is not based on the vote cast
at the last preceding election, but on the enrollment. In six hundred out of the 1,392 election
districts of New York the enrollment of Nov.
23rd, 1895, was larger than the Republican vote
cast at the election just previous. Thus is the
cornerstone of representative government crum-
bling away.

It is upon this sham enrollment that the bossism of the Empire State relies to secure dele-
gations to national conventions, secure cabinet
positions and control of the treasury and administration of our country. The same system
is in vogue in nearly every large city in our
country. It is employed from Maine to California. In San Francisco a boss has returned from
an exile enforced by criminal indictment by the
grand jury, to resume his operations as political
dictator. The means employed in carrying on

criminal politics are so reprehensible that honest men shrink therefrom, and rogues must necessarily be relied upon.

Again blind Boss Buckley has a firm hold on the political machine of the Democratic party in San Francisco. What a commentary on our primary election system that such men should be able to manipulate it! The reform needed all over this nation is the purification of the primary. Until that is done all talk about clean politics and government responsible to the people is absurd vaporing. The only uniformity in the primary laws at present, is that they uniformly confirm the powers of the bosses. By a primary election, which he controls and manipulates, the boss first forms the general committee of the party in his city or country. Then all future primaries and nominating conventions are in his control. The only way to beat him is to beat the party, and that the average American is not prone to do. By his control of the general committee, the boss has it absolutely in his power to control the party registration and to determine who shall, and who shall not, belong to the party. Buckley in San Francisco and Platt in New York play the same game. In both states the law specially recognizes the custom of boss organization as something sacred.

We safeguarded the ballot, but we leave the making up of the ticket printed on that ballot to those selfishly and often corruptly interested in politics.

Examination of the laws regulating primaries in several states that have attempted legislation reveals the fact that the few laws enacted for that purpose so far have been drawn up more to protect the managers of political machines than to protect the people.

In several states the laws are deliberately drawn to absolutely deprive the citizen of all power of choice. He has as little control over the making of the ticket he is expected to vote, as he has over the tides of the sea. With a constantly increasing number of elective offices, the power of bossism under corrupt primaries is rapidly multiplying.

THE CALIFORNIA STATUTE.

THE California act of 1895, providing for "a general primary election, to promote the purity thereof, by regulating the conduct thereof, and to support the privileges of free suffrage thereat, prohibiting certain acts and practices in relation thereto, and providing for the punishment thereof," is the most perfect piece of legislature yet devised on this subject. The title of the act tells the whole story of this most needed reform.

It requires all political parties to hold primaries on the second Tuesday in July preceding the election, at the same place and hour, and at public expense.

Any political party that polled three per cent of the entire vote can hold a primary election under this act.

The county election commissioners in January select, in the same manner as a jury is drawn, the names of judges of the primaries from a list of not less than thirty electors of each precinct and publish the same, the names to be divided equally among the several political parties.

Twenty days before the primary there is drawn from the list in each precinct and published a name for inspector, two judges and two clerks, representing the several parties.

The primary officers are sworn, their duties prescribed, their services paid by the county, and the primary election for delegates or candidates of all parties is held at the same time and place in each voting precinct, each party voting in a different box, but all voting on one ballot on the Australian plan, printed and furnished at public expense. The polls are open all day, the ballots are carefully counted and preserved in the presence of bystanders, and the whole result is certified in duplicate and safeguarded as perfectly as the regular election.

The general primary for presidential electors shall be held on the last Tuesday in March in the same manner. It requires that political primaries of all parties be held, and at the same time and place after due advertisement. This is the first essential, as it prevents repeating and stimulates a show of the full strength of each party, and brings out the fullest competition for nominations. It requires that the election commissioners of each county select names from the assessment roll of each precinct, divided equally between the different parties, and from these are chosen by lot the judges who act at the common primaries. This takes out of the power of the boss the selection of the officers who conduct the primary and certify the result more often to their liking than according to the actual result. The new law then goes further and prescribes that the canvass must be public, and in the presence of the bystanders, the voters of each party voting directly for their choice of candidates or delegates in separate ballot-boxes for each party, and having their name and residence recorded on separate tally sheets. The tickets are required to be strung, numbered, sealed and preserved until after all the state conventions are held, and all frauds are as carefully safeguarded against, and as severely punished, as in the Australian ballot law. The law has been declared invalid on some technicality, but the text of the Court's decision is not yet made public. Press reports say this just and wise measure was thrown out by the Court because it was made to apply only to counties of the first and second class, a defect that was probably well known to be fatal by some of the lawyers in the legislature that passed it. So the people are thrown back on the old Porter primary law of 1865-6 and its amendments, about as crude, defective and easily manipulated by those against whom it is supposed to protect society, as any law can be constructed. There is one officer who opens, canvasses and certifies the return of the primary. The party central committee calls the primary and conducts it, the ballots are not preserved, and aside from its general reputation as a heavenly country, California is entitled to be called the paradise of the boss so far as the laws making it easy for him to operate at slate-making and convention packing are concerned. It is doubtful if a people so long accustomed to loosely conducted primaries would have taken much advantage of the new law.

While the new California act is suspended in the courts, it must be remembered that most states have no law to regulate the primary. In the few states having such laws it will be found they are fatally defective, or designedly drawn to throw power into the hands of the bosses. A primary law that leaves the selection of the officers in each precinct to the party central committee, or that leaves the primary open only to previously enrolled members of a party, or that requires no preservation of the ballots cast, is of this class. In one state the bosses have gone so far as to secure a primary law where the voter must receive his ticket direct from the hands of the boss-appointed primary officials, and shall vote no other.

As a result of unprotected and easily corrupted primaries, statistics show that while the debt of all the states and territories has decreased $26,-195,462 from 1890 to 1895, the debt of our fifty largest cities has increased from $465,610,739 to $565,665,539 in the same period. While the state and national debt has decreased, the debt of cities, where corrupt politics are the worst, has increased over $100,000,000. The increased debt in all municipalities for the ten years preceding was only $40,000,000. (See figures by J. K. Upton, *Harper's Weekly*, Jan. 11.) What is the remedy? A comparison of the present methods of conducting the primaries in New York or any of our larger cities, with the new California law, should point out the way to reform.

The primary must be placed beyond the control of the selfishly interested office-holding and office-seeking class. The power to make nominations must be placed in the hands of the masses of each party, where it belongs. Thus alone can government become responsible to the governed, and without this there can be no just or good government. The principle that obtains in THE OLD CRAWFORD SYSTEM still in vogue in many of the older states, and practiced in some of the largest counties and cities

of Ohio, Illinois and Iowa, cannot be much im-
proved upon. It can be perfected and the result
safeguarded and made as sure and certain to do
its work as the Australian ballot. Under the
old Crawford system there was no delegate
county convention. In each precinct the party
voters cast a ballot direct for their choice of
candidates for office within the party. The
primaries are held all over the county on the same
day, and are conducted like a general election.
If there are six candidates for nomination for
representative, sheriff, or any county office, the
voter marks his man for each office, and the
candidate for nomination receiving the largest
vote throughout the county is the party candidate for election. This is a simple and direct
plan of nominating. It is said that it is cumber-
some, expensive and old-fashioned. But it can
not be tampered with and corrupt combinations
are impossible.

Under the Crawford system, candidates for
congress and delegates to state conventions are
chosen in the same way.

The people of the United States will never
have a representative or responsible Democratic
form of government until they destroy the present system of political corruption, which, with
its roots in the congested populations of our

large cities, extends its branches into everv hamlet of our country.

Billion-dollar congresses, irresponsible legislatures, boodle aldermen, corporation corruption, boss-ridden administration, or clean, decent, intelligent government—which?

Which shall our country become, Christian or Cossack? Government of, by, and for the disinterested masses, or a highly organized plutocrat paternalism?

THE PRIMARY AND CITY POLITICS.

No discussion of bossism in American politics can be satisfactory without a parallel consideration of the primary system under which it flourishes. Bossism and machine politics exist simply because they can, not because they are indispensable, just as slavery and piracy flourished, until the laws of nations rendered those institutions impossible.

American politics, as now existing, is an anomaly of highly perfected law at one end, and perfect barbarism at the other, which is unfortunately the beginning. By the Australian system we protect the freedom, the purity, the secrecy and the perfect equality of all votes cast, so far as it is possible for human ingenuity to accomplish that result. The party primary and the nomination convention we leave unguarded, or, what is worse, guarded by the thieves and corruptionists who prey off the body politic.

The voter at the ballot-box is not the unit of our political system, as we fondly suppose. The ballot-box is not the place where the people register their decrees as to who shall govern them, or what that government shall be. The unit of the government is the party voter who goes, often for hire or at the best for selfish solicitation, to the precinct primary and votes for delegates to the county convention. The citizen at the ballot-box only ratifies the decree of the slate-makers at the primaries. He has the option of defeating their ticket at the polls, but he uses that opportunity so rarely that the exception proves the rule.

As twenty-eight millions of the American people are now gathered in cities, where the more or less corruptly managed party primary is the dominant force in municipal, state and national politics, the question arises, if the unit of all our political activities be contaminated, if the fountains of our politics are impure and unpatriotic, how can the result be otherwise than a disappointment and a failure? The primary is the lever with which the boss lifts the world of American politics.

The question of bossism is of peculiar interest to the people of the Pacific coast states. It is a system with the result of which they are only too familiar. What is the situation? Large states with a thinly scattered population, having a congestion of city population in one county, afford a perfect paradise for bossism. In the

states of California, Oregon, Washington and
Utah, the boss in politics is in clover. His
methods are the same, though the manifestations
are different. Bossism in its various phases may
be said to have its corrupting grasp on these
four states as firmly as on the politics of the older
Eastern states, with the exception in its favor,
that here on the coast it meets with less opposition and less organized resistance. It has almost
an unrestrained scope for its operations, and
its hold-ups of the tax-payer are as regular and
systematic as those of a well organized gang of
highwaymen on a line of stages through a thinly
settled mountain region.   .

As in gambling and stage robbing, on the
Pacific coast, the stakes are larger, so the game
of politics here yields the largest prizes. The
boss pays no attention to peanut politics. He
aims at the control of the most profitable departments of city government, the management of
an entire state administration, the making of
United States senators and congressmen, the
control of the supreme court, the appointment
of federal judges and the nomination of the *nisi
prius* judges. Through the latter he secures the
appointment of receivers, who in turn, if he hap-
pens to be a good lawyer, employ him as counsel,
or turn entire corporations over to him as sole

referee. Thus the skillful manipulation of ward politics by a city boss enables him to become almost a commercial dictator, and when a period of depression sweeps over the country, other men's losses are his gains, and he comes out of the storm with a smiling face and a well-filled pocketbook.

The civil service reformers of our country have been complaining of the evils of bossism and machine politics for twenty years, and the country enters upon the presidential campaign more completely dominated by both than ever before in the history of our country. Occasionally a stray minister of the gospel like Parkhurst, or an accidental "moral waver" has arisen to stem the tide for a few years, until the oncoming waves of corruption have again swept over him, and washed away his works of reform, just as bossism and Tammany have again clasped hands over the grave of the good government in New York City.

What is the remedy? An uprising of patriotism and intelligent protest on the part of the average voter, a demand for the right to a voice in the government of parties and also of schools, city, county, state and nation, is first needed. Second, this awakening of the moral sentiment and the instinct of political self-preservation

against corruption must be crystallized into a
national primary law as carefully safeguarded
as the general election laws. Every member
of every party must have the right to vote directly for his choice among those who aspire to
candidacy for every office on the ticket. The
primaries of all parties must be held on the same
day, at the same place, and at public expense.
These propositions may seem revolutionary to
some, but without a revolution there is nothing
but a failure ahead of us, and possibly dissolution of the republic.

Why? Because bossism means government by
the worst and in the most expensive manner. It
means organized and perpetually increasing extravagance in public affairs and a closer and
closer alliance between the selfish, the criminal
and governing classes who unite to prey off the
producers of wealth and the taxpayer. This
may seem a strong statement, but let a fearless
and intelligent examination be made and it will
lead to no other conclusion. Government by
the people has been the failure that it is, because
its very inception is tainted with selfishness and
fraud.

Let us consider the ordinary method of operation by a political boss in a city of fifty to one
hundred thousand. His first battle is to get

control of the party central committee. Having that, he has the right to call primaries and conventions in the city and country. As will be shown, in the absence of laws to safeguard the primaries, this means a great deal. It gives him control of their conduct from organization to certifying their result. He has the selection of the judges and clerks and the control of the registry and the return, as well as the disposition of the ballots cast at the primary. This gives him the power to man these nominating elections with his tools, to vote the occupants of cheap boarding houses, the frequenters of saloons, and any number of voters colonized for the purpose from other cities, or even from different parts of the same city where they are not needed for his purposes, and return any delegates he pleases. This is what is done by the boss in the absence of all laws to govern the primaries, and his power to make slates and control the county convention there is none dares dispute. But his work is done still more effectively by means of laws drawn for the apparent purpose of regulating the primaries, but in reality to clinch his powers over the same with the semblance of legal authority; enacted ostensibly to protect the public, but in reality to rivet the chains of bossism all the tighter.

A growing public sentiment against machine politics in general, and dictation to the party and the people by the office-looting classes in particular, has compelled the enactment of some laws for the regulation of the primaries.

But any political boss is sharp enough to see that a reform at the primaries, that would take away from him the power to slate delegates and make up a ticket in the interest of office-holders or office-seekers who will do his bidding, would retire him to private life. So he hedges and himself secures his calling by the adoption of a law that is apparently constructed to purify the primary and abolish machine politics, but in reality it blinds the honest intentioned citizen with a mask of legal formality behind which bossism carries on its work of corruption in greater security.

PRIMARY ELECTION LAWS.

THE primary election laws of the Pacific coast states are worthy of a brief study. The territory of Utah, now entered upon statehood, has no primary law. But the bosses of the Eastern states have had their hands on the politics of Utah, and it was early given out that all the arrangements had been perfected to organize the state, and elect senators who should be truly representative of the interests of the big corporation machine that runs the politics of the federal courts and the Pacific railroad. If they have their way, Utah will enter the sisterhood of states with her hands tied behind her, and as far as possible from being governed by political power emanating directly from the masses of the people. A curious situation came about at Ogden last fall in the city primaries. The Republican committee issued a call setting forth that at the city primaries to be held October 14th, all Republicans in each precinct would vote directly for candidates for city officials, and that the candidate having the highest number of votes in all the wards would be the candidate of the party at the coming election. The committee appointed the judges, selected the usual places for voting, announced the rules governing challenges, and thus did away with the old machine-method of electing a slate of delegates in each ward who then hold a city convention and make the ticket for the Republicans of the city. The committee no doubt intended to do the right thing, and were animated by a desire to give the people a direct voice in the selection of the candidates for the city offices.   But they overreached in naming the judges of the primary, giving but two days' time to consider the merits of the aspirants for nomination for mayor and the other offices to be filled.   The cry of "slate" was raised against the well-meaning city committee, and their plan was overthrown, and the old way of electing delegates to a city convention was adopted. Extending the time for holding the primaries on the new method one week did not meet the objection of the conservative machine politicians, who insisted on the old way of making up a slate of delegates in each ward; and so the first attempt at placing the nominating power directly in the hands of the rank and file of the party was defeated, and the old abuses perpetuated.

Washington enacted no primary law until 1890, and then it was not made obligatory upon any party. The first section recited that the law should only apply; "whenever any committee or body authorized by the rules or customs of such political association *shall elect to accept and act under its provisions.*" The law also allowed the party central committee to name the judges and clerks of the primaries. This law is superseded by the act of 1895, "to regulate the holding of primaries," which also is not obligatory, the party managers being permitted to hold open primaries if they choose to do so. There have been no primaries held under this act at this date, but experience will show that it is most cunningly constructed in the interests of the bosses and the machine, and to deprive the disinterested and patriotic partisan of all possible freedom of choice, as to who shall represent him in conventions. All the evils of the old caucus are legalized. A caucus called by the central committee chooses the officers and clerks of the primary. The law declares that at this caucus, to be held previous to the primary, there shall be selected a list of at least twice as many delegates as shall be elected by the primary. These names shall be printed and "shall be the only ballot voted," and to make sure of no interference with the caucus ticket, the law provides that this ticket "shall be obtained only by the voter *from the primary election officers immediately before voting.*" It is true that under this law the party voter will have his choice of at least two times as many names as there are delegates to be elected at the primary, but these names are all chosen at a caucus which is entirely out of his control and may be held in a saloon or the back office of a ward boss without any legality or publicity. The provisions as to counting the ballots at the primary and keeping a record of the same, are very stringent and will be observed to the letter. The slate-makers are not such fools as to violate the non-essentials of their trade, when they have the essentials all in their own hands—the making of the slates, the prohibition of any independent voting, and the counting and certifying of the result. Are not such laws the triumph of American political ingenuity?

An attempt to discuss the boss in California politics would be to write the political history of the state. The recent struggles of *Blind Boss Buckley* to regain his prestige in San Francisco politics are worthy of more notice than the editorials of the daily press have given them. The subject is probably so worn and hackneyed that no attention would be paid to whatever might be said. And then the boss and his assistants are as indifferent to the press and public opinion as they are to the public welfare. As there is no such thing as just and equitable party management under the bossism, so there is no way to manage the boss himself, through the ordinary channels of public influence. He is not amenable to the law, because there is no law to restrain him. He cannot be disciplined by the party, because he is king in its councils. He is not responsible to the people, because they are the mere dupes that ratify his works. Our politics results in free self-government of, by and for the people only in theory, but an irresponsible despotism in practice. So long as the people are blind to this fact they will grope about for remedies, and curse bossism. But there it will end. As California was one of the first states to adopt ballot reform, we may hope, when the people are aroused to the real cause of their thralldom to bossism, they will just as quickly apply the remedy and purify the primary. An effort to that end was made in the last legislature and the most perfect primary election law yet invented was passed, but it is being resisted in the courts.

The Oregon law for the regulation of prima-

ries was passed in 1891. It was drawn by the
then most conspicuous political boss in the
state. He was given *carte blanche* by prominent men of wealth, and bankers, to draw on
them for all the expenses necessary to pack the
primaries for his slates, by rounding up the
boarding house and slum vote. With these slates
he went into the county convention and as a
chairman of the county committee nominated the
temporary chairman of the convention, who in
turn drew from his pockets the committees on
credentials, resolutions, and temporary organization. The temporary chairman, afterwards
made permanent, appointed three tellers, who
were creatures of the boss, and if the convention
did not ratify the slate of the boss, it was the
duty of these tellers to see that the proper men
were counted in. This made the domination of
the Portland boss absolute over the primaries
and nominating convention. The only exception to his sway was the sheriff's office, the fees
and emoluments of which were so large that a
strong man could set up a machine of his own
and elect himself cheaper than the boss could,
and has generally done so. But the office cost
the people all the more for that. But it was not
the disposition of the city and county offices that
the boss cared most about. The power to make

the legislative ticket and control its vote, and
therewith make senators (who in turn nominate
federal judges for life), and passage of city
charter bills, was far more coveted, the former
enabling him to control federal patronage and
the latter giving him the means to keep control
of the city government,and in turn by contracts
recover for the capitalists and bankers the money
first advanced to carry the primaries and insure
the election of the not always popular characters
on the boss's ticket. The sale of bridges and
ferries, the letting of water-works contracts, and
sale of millions of bonds completed the circle of
spoils politics.

What was more proper than that city politicians who had been conducting politics success-
fully and profitably from this standpoint, should
draw up and pass a bill to protect and regulate
the primaries? The Oregon primary election
law will be found to be all that might be expected, considering its source. It applies only
to cities of 2,500 or over, and only to city elections. The party central committee must publish a call setting forth the purpose of the primary to be held, the date, places, hours to be
open, number of delegates and three judges for
each precinct, who appoint two clerks. This
leaves the whole organization in the hands of the

same committee that makes the slates. If the judges appointed do not show up, five of the crowd present may name them. The record of the primary is preserved in duplicate and one copy filed with the county clerk. That seems a fair proposition, but when it is considered that the ballots are not preserved and no one is even supposed to have them, it will be seen that whatever list of names the officers see fit to report as having voted is final, and there is no possibility of going behind the return they make. They can absolutely count in any slate of delegates they see fit, and there is no recourse.

This law has only been used a few times, and has not been a protection to the primaries. It has not prevented bossism and corruption in the city of Portland, as it was not intended for that purpose. It simply tended to confirm the dictatorship of one-man power, against which last year there was a perfect revolution within the dominant party. The revolution was sufficient to compel the adoption of a reform platform, bring new men to the front for state offices, and the people were promised a new deal and relief from the legislature. But with the hold-over senators the boss was able to organize the senate, make himself its master and defeat every measure of reform.

RESULTS IN SOME CITIES.

ONE way to get at the true state of political morality in a given community, is to take the accounts from all the newspapers over a period of great excitement following the bursting of one of the carbuncles of corruption. By applying the principles of what might be termed the comparative criminology of politics, the observer need not be led far astray. In the Pacific coast cities are gathered the sharpest politicians from the various overcrowded schools of activity in the East. The native spoilsman can hold his own with imported talent. The graduates of criminal maladministration form an alumni society whose class motto is: "To prey upon the public is a legitimate occupation." In private they appear to be business men, and one of their catch phrases is, that "public affairs must be con ducted on a business basis." In their private conversation they are not adverse to plain speaking. They say: "Who goes into politics except for money? Nobody but a fool, and he don't last long. Everybody is in politics for what there is in it." Men entertaining such ideas are

sent into the city council, hold city offices, sit
on the board of education, go to the legislature,
and occupy the state and judicial offices.   Is
it any wonder that with such principles animat-
ing an aggressive and numerous class of political
sharpers, and with no safeguards thrown about
the primaries and nominating conventions,
some of our best Pacific coast cities should be
on the verge of bankruptcy, honeycombed with
corruption and staggering under a burden of
extravagant officialism?   Seattle has a debt of
five millions and an interest charge of $750
a day. Tacoma has as yet only the beginnings
of a water-works system, costing now $2,080,-
000, that a good authority says is worth $350,000.
Portland has a debt in round numbers of five
millions of dollars.   In Tacoma one of the
bursted banks is said to have on its books an
item of $18,000 disbursed as election expenses
to secure the re-election of one Boggs, a de-
faulter but recently convicted, and now in jail,
under whose skillful management $300,000 dis-
appeared. Boggs was the party candidate of the
bosses, and of the banks to whom he afterwards
turned over the public moneys. Torchlight pro-
cessions a mile long paraded the streets to make
sure his re-election after it was known that his
affairs were in disorder. A few months later he
disappeared.

Bossism in cities of solid, substantial growth is bad enough. But when spoils politics is united with political banking in a boom town, the result is chaos and municipal anarchy. Within sixty days the city government of Tacoma collapsed in bankruptcy. In times of depression, when well-managed governments become a source of financial stability to the business community, having the property of the tax-payers for resources, the extravagance and corruption bred of bossism leads to dissolution. In Tacoma the methods of concealment, secret corruption and hidden debauchery in municipal politics have had full sway. The result is pathetic for American citizens to contemplate. The City of Destiny, the terminus of Oriental traffic and trans-continental railways, where the Northern Pacific railroad has lavished millions to make a city, is now suffering under the humiliation of absconded officials, suspended banks, an empty treasury and a blackened reputation. A recent showing by a special committee of the city council is little more than an inventory of public funds that are vanished, empty vaults, plundered safes, cash drawers rifled, and boxes full of the wortless "I. O. U.'s" of still more worthless politicians. The last money had been drawn out on mere cash-tickets marked with the

names of the favorites and pets who had a pull
on the city treasurer. With what bitter irony he
must have said to himself, "Are they not my
friends political? How can I refuse them?"
balances in suspended banks $584,630.79!
These fellows who follow a spoils politics are
accurate to the cent in keeping account of the
vanished funds of the tax-payer. When the receiver took charge of one of the banks he found
$1.10 cash. The account books and cashier
were missing. Only the day before the city
government thought it had $58,000 on deposit.
The letter of an Eastern capitalist who had
$100,000 invested in Tacoma, and who had
boundless faith in the exceptional situation and
natural resources of the city, becomes pathetic
when he concludes: "I tell you frankly that the
odor of politics in Tacoma is not savory, and it
is a terrible drawback to the prosperity of the
place." Dear Mr. Capitalist of the Bay State,
are not your municipal governments, too, honeycombed with jobbery, fraud and corruption?
Have you the grace to point to the cities of the
West and say their government is not right—is
not business?

POLITICAL BANKING.

IF the truth were known in every instance it would be found that the majority of banking institutions in cities of 25,000 to 100,000 population, that went to the wall in the United States in the panic of 1893-94, were closely connected with municipal politics. Of the $19,000,000 of these robberies and defalcations in 1893, and the $25,000,000 in 1894, it would be found that they were the direct results of the bankers entering the field of machine politics. To do this requires money, plenty of it, and the spending of it freely, the carrying of spurious paper and the floating of questionable loans on corporations connected with the public service,such as water bonds, street-car mortgages,gas stock, and electric-light plants. By securing favorable contracts through the political creatures of bossism, extensions are planned and carried out that afterwards prove unremunerative, and the stock and securities of the entire plant are weakened and thrown on the market.

Bossism in city-government does its work in a circle. In the largest cities the circuit is formed with the boss at one. end and the vicious and criminal classes at the other. In the smaller cities above referred to, at various points in the circle are stationed the heeler, the boss, the office-holder, the tax-gatherer, and the political banker. The latter advances the money to defray the expenses of packing the primaries. The money is dispensed by the boss, who then sees to it that the office-holder make enough out of the public service, which is collected from the tax-payer, to enable the political banker to recoup himself, with big interest. When the panic came on, it found many banking institutions carrying large quantities of speculative paper and municipal warrants against either the city, county, school or state treasury. As liquidations proceeded the political banks were crowded to the wall. In the city of Portland, Oregon, not less than five suspended, two of which resumed under new management. The other three are still closed, or in the hands of receivers, with hundreds of thousands of dollars of public funds unaccounted for. Of course the boss sees to it that one of his pets is appointed receiver, and what could not be stolen by machine politics now disappears under the guise of law. The half-dozen banks that recently collapsed in Tacoma owed their failure entirely to municipal corruption. They have been holding on by the eye-lids since the panic of two years ago, kept alive by continuous deposits of public moneys. Three hundred thousand dollars obtained from the sale of water bonds was stolen in a lump by one of these banks. Goaded by public sentiment, the corrupt public officials were at last compelled to demand the public money, and the banks closed their doors. Their final collapse is held by banking circles as marking a new era, but the political situation remains unchanged. The political bank may go out of existence, but the politician who banks on plundering the tax-payer is still "doing business at the old stand." There are now but five commercial banks in Tacoma, two of which are national, and one of which is doing one-third of the entire business of the community, as shown by the clearing house re-turns. It has not a dollar of public funds on deposit, it being the policy of the bank not to receive such deposits. Further than this, no officer of the bank is a surety on the bond of a public officer. So damaging is the reputation of being connected with municipal politics, as now conducted, that the banking institutions known to receive favors from public officials in the way of deposits on public funds are looked upon with distrust. The character of the transactions necessary in conducting-political banking is such as to undermine the ordinary dictates of prudence, necessary to success. The extravagance and corruption of bossism in the city government is so repugnant to business principles that banking institutions, which must be conducted on a high plane of integrity to succeed at all, are the first to suffer from the contamination of politics.

What is the remedy? Until the conduct of the primary election is rigidly safeguarded by law and the expense thereof is borne by the state, large sums of money will be necessary to hold the primaries of the different parties in large cities. This money will be advanced by capitalists, and it is quite natural that banks receiving favors from politicians should be called upon to furnish the required capital. Public sentiment will restrain political banking, and public sentiment must compel protection and purification of the primary.

www.ingramcontent.com/pod-product-compliance
Lightning Source LLC
Chambersburg PA
CBHW021529270326
41930CB00008B/1165